American Quilter's Society
2008
Catalogue
of
Show Quilts

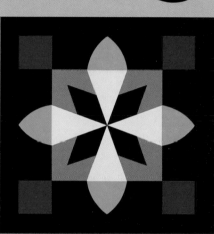

Semi-finalists in the
24th Annual

Quilt Show & Contest

PADUCAH · AQS · KENTUCKY

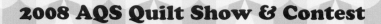
Located in Paducah, Kentucky, the American Quilter's Society (AQS) is dedicated to promoting the accomplishments of today's quilters. Through its publications and events, AQS strives to honor today's quiltmakers and their work and to inspire future creativity and innovation in quiltmaking.

Artwork © 2008, American Quilter's Society

EXECUTIVE EDITOR: NICOLE C. CHAMBERS
EDITOR: BONNIE K. BROWNING
GRAPHIC DESIGN: ELAINE WILSON
COVER DESIGN: MICHAEL BUCKINGHAM
PHOTOGRAPHY: SUPPLIED BY THE INDIVIDUAL QUILTMAKERS

American Quilter's Society
P. O. Box 3290 • Paducah, KY 42002-3290
www.AmericanQuilter.com

Additional copies of this book may be ordered from the American Quilter's Society, PO Box 3290, Paducah, KY 42002-3290, or online at www.AmericanQuilter.com.

Proudly printed and bound in the United States of America

The quilts entered in this year's AQS Quilt Contest represent a variety of themes, from beautiful florals and finely detailed animals in appliqué to exquisite pieced work. Technology continues to have an influence on the quilts, with two-thirds of them being quilted by machine. This year we received more quilts that were quilted by hand – thank you to those who continue the tradition of fine hand quilting.

Quilters are extending the use of threadwork, embroidery, and painting to larger pieces. Quilts featuring vivid color schemes abound in the wall art categories.

Quilters from 46 U.S. states and 13 countries entered this year's contest.

Make your plans now to enter the 2009 AQS 25th Anniversary Quilt Contest.

Meredith Schroeder

Meredith Schroeder
AQS President and Founder

101, Aunt MiMi's Flower Garden, 83" x 83"
Elsie M. Campbell, Dodge City, KS

102, Angel's Trumpet, 93" x 93"
Barbara J. Clem, Rockford, IL

Angel's Trumpet pattern, *100 Appliqué Quilt Patterns* by Jan Halgrimson, Weaver-Finch Publications

103, Reminiscence, 74" x 90"
Lauren C. DeVantier, Amherst, NY

104, Pots de Fleurs, 85½" x 86"
Kathy Delaney, Overland Park, KS

Reminiscence by Lydia Quigley, The Rabbit Factory

105, PRELUDE OF ROSSE, 84" x 84"
Masako Kumagawa,
Agatuma, Gunma, Japan

106, LAHAINA PINEAPPLE, 89" x 106"
Midori Nagatani, Gotemba, Shizuoka, Japan

107, LEA'S CHOICE, 82" x 82"
Joanie Zeier Poole, Sun Prairie, WI

108, HAWAIIAN GINGERS, 82" x 90"
Yoko Sakaguchi, Setagaya, Tokyo, Japan

Inspired by 1937 central medallion in *Twentieth Century Quilts, 1900–1950* by Thomas K. Woodard and Blanche Greenstein, E. P. Dutton

Kathy Nakajima class

109, Spirit of Mother Earth, 99" x 99"
Sharon Schamber, Payson, AZ

110, Joy, 89" x 89"
Marilyn Smith, Columbia, MO

111, For the Love of Lilies, 91" x 106"
Ruth V. Smith, New Port Richey, FL

112, Image of Autumn, 82" x 80"
Mildred Sorrells, Macomb, IL

The Country Lily Quilt by Cheryl A. Benner and Rachel T. Pellman, Good Books www.goodbks.com

Delirious pattern, Karen K. Stone Quilts by Karen K. Stone, Electric Quilt Co.

Pride of Iowa block, Patterns for EQ Software: 1920s & 1930s' Blocks, Electric Quilt Company

113, SPRING OF DESIRE, 80" x 80"
Ted Storm-vanWeelden,
's-Gravenzande, Netherlands

201, THE TIGER, 92½" x 116½"
Marilyn Bujalski, Clear Lake, MN

202, CABIN FEVER, 80" x 80"
Susie Dumas, Macon, GA

203, SHADOWS OF UMBRIA, 83" x 83"
Diane Gaudynski, Waukesha, WI

Walking Tiger™ pattern, *Animals in Cross Stitch* by Jayne Netley-Mayhew and Nicki Wheeler, David and Charles Publishers

Antique Log Cabin pattern by Julie Hendrecksen, *American Patchwork and Quilting,* April 2005

Block from Stellar Delight pattern, Johanna Wilson

Inspired by an 1855 antique quilt

204, LOST IN ENGLAND, 96" x 96"
Cindy Vermillion Hamilton
Pagosa Springs, CO

205, BIRDS AROUND MY WINDOW, 92" x 92"
Terri Krysan, Lakeville, MN

206, LOG CABIN STARS, 78" x 94"
Scott A. Murkin, Asheboro, NC

207, BIG BIRD BLUES, 84" x 84"
Claudia Clark Myers & Marilyn Badger
Duluth, MN

Kansas City *Star* newspaper

208, Log Cabin/Kaleidoscope Two (II)
88" x 88", Fumiko Ohkawa, Kobe, Japan

209, Redaction, 76" x 91"
Loretta A. Painter, Norris, TN

210, Blue & White Rhapsody, 91" x 91"
Ann T. Pigneri, Louisville, KY

211, Ribbon Stars, 88" x 106"
Amy Reitzel, Ottawa Lake, MI

Based on *Anniversary Stars,* from *40 Fabulous Quick-Cut Quilts* by Evelyn Sloppy, Martingale & Co.

Flannel Star by Brenda Henning, Bear Paw Productions

East to Eden pattern, *The Quilt Design Workbook* by Beth and Jeffrey Gutcheon, Simon and Schuster Trade

212, Mamaw's Puzzle, 78" x 89½"
Valli Schiller, Naperville, IL

213, Midnight Lady, 86½" x 87"
Sharyl L. Schlieckau, Loganville, WI

214, Stepping Out in Color, 68" x 88"
Kathryn Sims, Alexis, IL

215, Victorian Valentine, 84" x 84"
Mary Sue Suit & Judy Woodworth, Sidney, NE

216, FEATHERED STAR II – SPRING, 71" x 82½"
Barbara Swinea, Fairview, NC

217, SKYROCKET, 77½" x 90¼"
Tess Thorsberg, Macon, GA

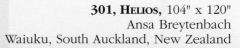

218, SPARKLERS & STARS, 99" x 99"
Renè Williams, Northridge, CA

301, HELIOS, 104" x 120"
Ansa Breytenbach
Waiuku, South Auckland, New Zealand

Skyrocket pattern, Scrap Frenzy: Even More Quick-Pieced Scrap Quilts by Sally Schneider, Martingale and Company

Simply Stars: Quilts That Sparkle by Alex Anderson, C&T Publishing; King-size Pineapple, Pineapple Quilt: A Piece of Cake by Loretta Smith, Quilt in a Day

Eagle design by Terry Thompson; Liberty Bell, *Designs on Freedom* by Bonnie K. Browning, American Quilter's Society; FLAGS OF THE AMERICAN REVOLUTION by Jan Patek, Girl Gang, Block-of-Month, 2007; Bay Window Quilt Shop patterns

302, LET FREEDOM RING, 86" x 86"
Dot Collins, Port Neches, TX

303, DRIFTING NOMADS, 98" x 118"
Georgan Ellerbruch, Brookings, SD

304, ONE TRIP TO BALTIMORE, 79" x 83"
Karen L. Guthrie, Marshall, MO

305, FAN-TASTIC FOLIAGE, 96" x 108"
Elisabeth Polenz Haase, Weston, WI

Heartland pattern by Pearl Pereira and Susan Prioleau, P3 Designs

Machine Quilt School with Yoko Ueda

Grand American Barn Garden, The Ultimate Half Log Cabin Book by Sharyn Craig, Chitra Publishing; Redwork Club: Designs by Betty Alderman, Cindy Taylor Oates, and Laurene Sinema

306, The Summer in My Memories, 67¼" x 82"
Masae Kashizaki, Yokohama, Kanagawa, Japan

307, One Stitch at a Time, 89" x 89"
Janet Knapp, Fergus Falls, MN

308, Dear Jane, 80" x 80"
Patricia Leeper, McAlester, OK

309, Geese in the Mountain Garden
86" x 86", Barbara E. Lies, Madison, WI

Dear Jane: The Two Hundred Twenty-five Patterns from the 1863 Jane A. Stickle Quilt by Brenda M. Papadakis, EZ Quilting by Wrights

Edge treatment inspired by Sharon Schamber

Kansas City Star and Kansas City Kansan newspaper patterns, 1930

310, La Vida es Sueño (Life Is a Dream)
74" x 80", Cecilia Macià Brewster, MA

311, Everything Old Is New Again, 83" x 83"
Kathy Munkelwitz & Nancy Sammis, Isle, MN

312, Awesome Blossoms, 94" x 94"
Claudia Clark Myers & Marilyn Badger
Duluth, MN

313, Autumn Returns, 84½" x 84½"
Gladi V. Porsche, Lee, NH

Inspired by the Dahlia pattern by Patricia Cox

314, IRISH CREAM, 84" x 84"
Linda M. Roy, Knoxville, TN

315, HIDAMARI, 72½" x 87¾"
Hiromi Sano, Tsuchiura, Japan

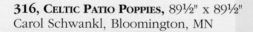

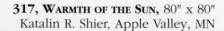

316, CELTIC PATIO POPPIES, 89½" x 89½"
Carol Schwankl, Bloomington, MN

317, WARMTH OF THE SUN, 80" x 80"
Katalin R. Shier, Apple Valley, MN

Poppies and Leaves, *Once Upon A Season* by Becky Goldsmith and Linda Jenkins, C&T Publishing, Inc.; *Bella Bella Quilts: Stunning Designs From Italian Mosaics* by Norah McMeeking, C&T Publishing, Inc.; *Celtic Quilting* by Gail Lawther, David and Charles Publishers, pages 20–21 and 115

Quilt Retreat with Ricky Tims

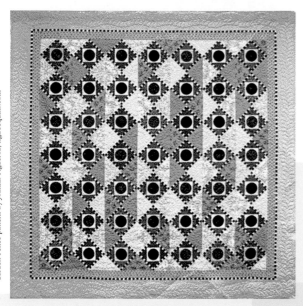

Garden Fence pattern by Joanna Figueroa, figtreequilts.com

Victorian Patterns and Designs in Full Color, G. A. and M. A. Audsley, Dover Pictorial Archives

318, Our Worlds, 108" x 108¾"
Lynda B. Smyth, Stittsville, Ontario, Canada

319, Cathedral Ceiling, 82" x 83"
Mildred Sorrells, Macomb, IL

320, Would You Kiss a Frog?, 91" x 91"
Patricia L. Styring, St. Augustine, FL

321, Polka Trip to Wien, 81½" x 81½"
Fusako Takido, Shimizu, Shizuoka, Japan

322, THE PADUCAH BLUE, 82⅓" x 82⅓"
Fumiko Tanabe, Ichihara, Chiba, Japan

Primrose Paths pattern from Fabric Trends for Quilters, *Issue 1, 2003; Fassing Fancy border:* Simple Traditions: 14 Quilts to Warm Your Home *by Kim Diehl, Martingale and Company*

323, LEAVING ON A SENTIMENTAL JOURNEY
104" x 104", Dee Van Driel, Fitchburg, WI

401, MEDIEVAL INSPIRATION, 69½" x 86"
Kathleen Burg, Sarasota, FL

402, STAR OF 2 SISTERS, 86" x 86"
Sonia Burgess & Gina Elias, Carol Stream, IL

Creative Medieval Designs for Appliqué by Eileen Campbell, Sally Milner Publishing Pty Ltd, distributed by Sterling Publishing Co., Inc.

Baltimore Beauties and Beyond: Studies in Classic Album Quilt Appliqué, Vol. 1 and Vol. 2 by Elly Sienkiewicz, C&T Publishing, Inc. *Artful Album Quilts: Appliqué Inspirations from Traditional Blocks* by Jane Townswick, Martingale and Company

Hawaiian Star by Judy and Bradley Niemeyer, Judy Niemeyer Quilting, Inc.

403, Butterflies Flew to Baltimore, 96½" x 81"
Marie Anne Coadic, Wilmington, NC

404, Shine On, 85" x 85"
Carol J. Cranston, Elkhorn, NE

405, The Poppies Quilt, 81" x 81"
Lauren C. DeVantier, Amherst, NY

406, Pussywillows, 64" x 82"
Tara Faughnan, Oakland, CA

The Poppies Quilt pattern, Primarily Patchwork, Australia

Wildflower Homestead pattern by Lois Worrell, *Quilters Newsletter Magazine*, December 1997

407, BUILDING A LIFE TOGETHER, 91" x 103"
Peggy Gelbrich, Yamhill, OR

408, BACK AT DARK: 30, 88" x 112"
Cynthia Hall, Asheville, NC

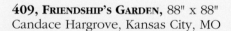

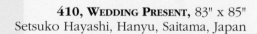

409, FRIENDSHIP'S GARDEN, 88" x 88"
Candace Hargrove, Kansas City, MO

410, WEDDING PRESENT, 83" x 85"
Setsuko Hayashi, Hanyu, Saitama, Japan

Friendship's Garden by Alma Allen and Cherie Ralston, Blackbird Designs

Kathy Nakajima class

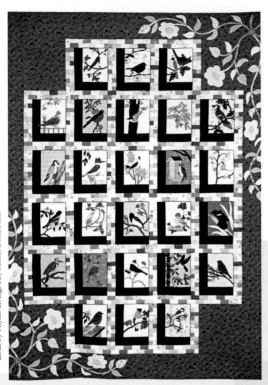

Hummingbird pattern, *Wild Birds: Designs for Appliqué and Quilting* by Carol Armstrong, C&T Publishing, Inc.; References: *Eastern Birds: Peterson Field Guides* by Roger Tory Peterson, Houghton Mifflin; *Attracting Birds* by Phyllis Elving, ed., Sunset Books, Inc.

411, BACKYARD SYMPHONY, 64" x 84"
Georgia M. Hayden, Union City, MI

412, BRODERIE PERSE ALBUM, 61" x 83"
Gerlinde Hruzek, Sun City West, AZ

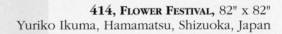

413, HAWAIIAN BOUQUET, 84" x 85"
Kumiko Iida, Minato, Tokyo, Japan

414, FLOWER FESTIVAL, 82" x 82"
Yuriko Ikuma, Hamamatsu, Shizuoka, Japan

Kathy Nakajima class

Noriko Masui class

415, HAWAIIAN ROYAL PATTERN, 83" x 83"
Masako Kato, Zushi, Kanagawa, Japan

416, SONG OF FLOWER, 92" x 92"
Jung Ran Kim, Seoul, South Korea

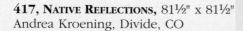

417, NATIVE REFLECTIONS, 81½" x 81½"
Andrea Kroening, Divide, CO

418, LADIES IN RED, 96" x 117"
Ona B. Mark, N. Huntingdon, PA

Masako Baba workshop

Magical Medallions pattern by Karen Kay Buckley

419, POLITE COMBINATION, 88" x 88"
Masako Masuzoe, Izumi, Osaka, Japan

420, ALMOST BALTIMORE, 83" x 83"
Ludmila Morgan, Lewes, DE

421, FABRIC FESTIVAL, 81¼" x 81¼"
Michiko Obuchi, Chiba City, Chiba, Japan

422, SILVER SWORD, 83" x 84"
Michiko Okada, Yokohama, Kanagawa, Japan

Kathy Nakajima class

423, A Spring Breeze, 76" x 84"
Rumiko Ooiwa, Tsukuba, Ibaraki, Japan

424, Rooted in Love, 87¼" x 103"
Peggy Parrott, Lakewood, CO

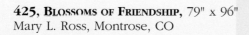

425, Blossoms of Friendship, 79" x 96"
Mary L. Ross, Montrose, CO

426, Blue Monstera, 81" x 94"
Yumiko Sato, Kokubunji, Tokyo, Japan

Delightful Quilts in Bloom by Mary L. Ross and Barbara Scheu, American Quilter's Society

Kathy Nakajima class

Kathy Nakajima class

The Wedding Star pattern by Judy Niemeyer, www.quiltworx.com

427, HAWAIIAN CROWN, 82" x 85"
Keiko Shimazaki, Chigasaki, Kanagawa, Japan

428, WEDDING STAR, 87" x 99"
Mindy Skinner, Lodi, WI

429, KAHILI, 83" x 86"
Kaori Takemori, Numazu, Shizuoka, Japan

430, MY DAUGHTER'S FAVORITE, 84" x 85"
Tomie Taniguchi, Izumi, Kanagawa, Japan

Kathy Nakajima class

Kathy Nakajima class

Log Cabin Wreath pattern by Virginia Robertson, Virginia Robertson Designs

431, IN MY LIFETIME, 76" x 94"
Marilyn Webert, St. Charles, MO

501, GARDEN FLOWERS, 98" x 108"
Marcelle Buttitta, Camarillo, CA

Kathy Nakajima class

432, FLOWERS OF HAWAII, 83" x 86"
Shihoko Yonamine, Koutou, Tokyo, Japan

502, SPRING SONG, 80" x 88"
Judy Cloe & Members of the
Birmingham Quilters Guild, Birmingham, AL

Berry Tree, *Appliqué Masterpiece: Little Brown Bird Patterns* by Margaret Docherty, American Quilter's Society; inspired by *Smashing Sets: Exciting Ways to Arrange Quilt Blocks* by Margaret Miller, C&T Publishing, Inc.; The Bonsai Tree, www.equilters.com; March, May and July, *Piecemakers Times and Seasons: A Calendar and Quilt Book,* Piecemakers; Friendship Tree and Tree patterns, *501 Quilt Blocks: A Treasury of Patterns for Patchwork and Appliqué* by Joan Lewis and Lynette Chiles, BHG, 1994, *Jacobean Applique: Book 2 - "Romantica"* by Patricia B. Campbell and Mimi Ayars, American Quilter's Society

503, TROPICAL SPLENDOR, 92" x 92"
The Feather Princesses – Tampa Chapter of
the Appliqué Society, Tampa, FL

504, BIRD'S PARADISE, 92" x 98"
Lehua Group, Saitama, Japan

505, REMEMBERING OZ, 76" x 85"
Karen Malone, Manhattan, KS

506, THE LITTLE ROSE GARDEN, 95" x 95"
Ozark Piecemakers Quilt Guild
Springfield, MO

Inspired by *Alice's Adventures in Wonderland* by Lewis Carroll, Walker Books

507, LE SOUVENIR DE ALICE, 79" x 85"
Misako Tsuru, Machida City, Tokyo, Japan

508, NINE-PATCHES FROM THE LADIES, 81½" x 86"
Dee Van Driel & 1999 Sioux Falls
Quilters' Guild Members, Fitchburg, WI

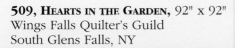

509, HEARTS IN THE GARDEN, 92" x 92"
Wings Falls Quilter's Guild
South Glens Falls, NY

510, FLOWER CIRCLE, 80" x 80"
Yufukobo Group, Matsusaka, Mie, Japan

Appliqué Masterpiece: Affairs of the Heart by Axe Rossmann, American Quilter's Society

Folk Art Primer Vol. 2, JoSonja's Inc.

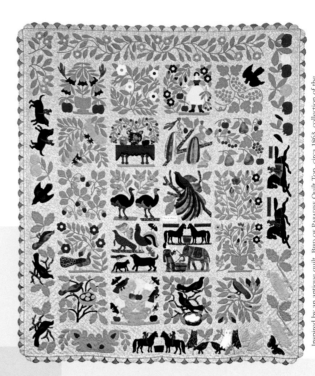

Inspired by an antique quilt, Bird of Paradise Quilt Top, circa 1863, collection of the American Folk Art Museum, New York City

601, Lovely Tenth Anniversary Rose, 81" x 81"
Yachiyo Katsuno, Setagaya, Tokyo, Japan

602, Lost Boy, 76" x 84"
Barbara Korengold, Chevy Chase, MD

603, A Slow Walk Through the Roses
83½" x 99", Diane M. Ladue, Beverly Hills, MI

604, Crystal Dreams, 88" x 87½"
Sandie Lush, Bristol, Avon, United Kingdom

Rose Sampler Supreme by Rosemary Makhan, Martingale & Co.; Red and Green: An Appliqué Tradition by Jeana Kimball, Martingale & Co.

Inspired by 1830s' quilt

605, STARDUST, 88" x 88"
Barbara Newman, Brandon, MS

606, TULIP GARDEN II, 64" x 82"
Hallie H. O'Kelley, Tuscaloosa, AL

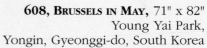

607, 267 BASKETS, 86½" x 86½"
Mary Owens, St. Louis, MO

608, BRUSSELS IN MAY, 71" x 82"
Young Yai Park,
Yongin, Gyeonggi-do, South Korea

Fruit Baskets, *The Classic American Quilt Collection: Baskets* by Mary V. Green and
Karen C. Soltys, ed., Rodale Press Inc.

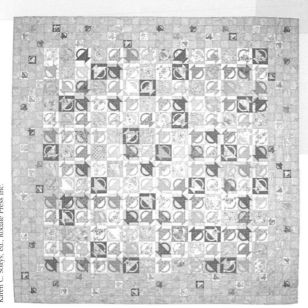

Patterns made from an antique quilt, circa 1850

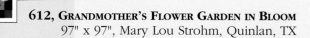

609, The Pastor's Attic, 95" x 96"
Marsha D. Radtke, Crossville, TN

610, Pennsylvania Palette, 85" x 85"
Wendy Caton Reed, Bath, ME

611, Spirit of the Sylvan Sun, 82½" x 84"
Kathryn J. Rouse, Racine, WI

612, Grandmother's Flower Garden in Bloom
97" x 97", Mary Lou Strohm, Quinlan, TX

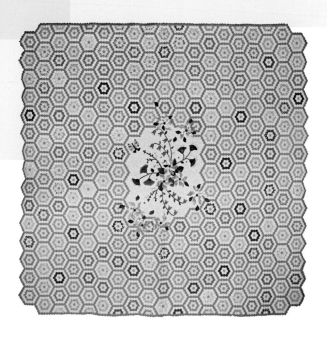

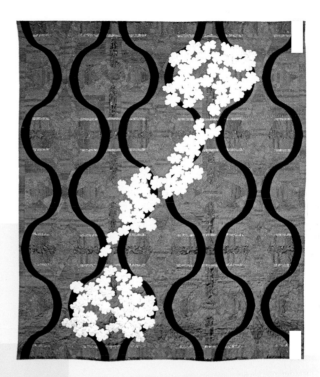

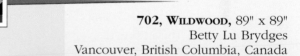

613, RAINBOW SEEKER, 84" x 84"
Michiko Takahashi, Hadano, Kanagawa, Japan

614, TATEWAKU — CLOUD OF FLOWERS, 67" x 80"
Naoko Yamada, Tajimi, Gifu, Japan

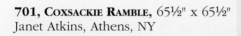

701, COXSACKIE RAMBLE, 65½" x 65½"
Janet Atkins, Athens, NY

702, WILDWOOD, 89" x 89"
Betty Lu Brydges
Vancouver, British Columbia, Canada

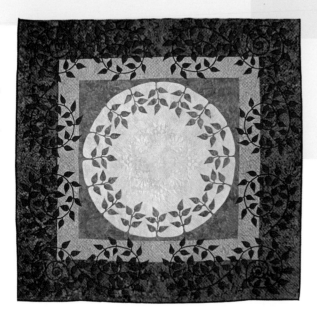

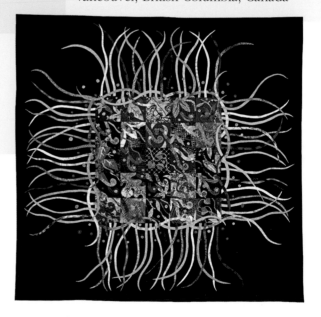

703, Night Jungle, 78" x 57"
Betty Busby, Albuquerque, NM

704, Antique Pomegranate, 68" x 68"
Carole Charles, Appleton, WI

705, Nifty Nine Patch, 68" x 68"
Robbi Joy Eklow, Third Lake, IL

706, Circus Stars, 86" x 86"
David D. Ewing, Richland Center, WI

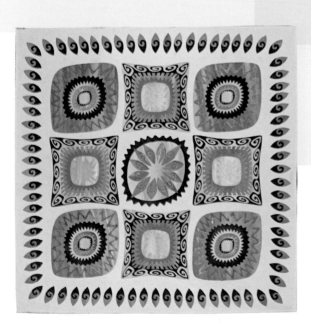

Antique Pomegranates pattern by Judy Flanagan, Quilter's Coop, Sanborn, IA

Inspired by *A Circus Bed Quilt* by Maxfield Parish, *Ladies Home Journal*, 1905

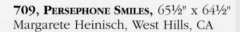

707, TREE O' LIFE, 62" x 65½"
Becky Goldsmith, Sherman, TX

708, PEONY DREAM MELODY, 68¼" x 70"
Molly Y. Hamilton-McNally, Tehachapi, CA

709, PERSEPHONE SMILES, 65½" x 64½"
Margarete Heinisch, West Hills, CA

710, AFRICAN ALBUM, 79" x 79"
Barbara Ann McCraw, Denton, TX

Inspired by appliqué blocks by Elly Sienkiewicz; a class with Susan Stiff

711, WISTFUL WILLOW (2008), 84" x 82"
Linda M. Roy, Knoxville, TN

712, MISSISSIPPI BACKROAD TREASURES
91" x 91", Judy Spiers, Foxworth, MS

713, SCOTTISH DANCE, 72" x 72"
Linda Steele, Park Orchards, Victoria, Australia

714, LIFE, 82" x 74"
Tamie Takahashi, Toyota, Aichi, Japan

712 Decorative Letters CD-ROM and Book (Dover Electronic Clip-Art), Dover Publications

Fairmeadow pattern by Jeana Kimball

715, ILLUMINATED ALPHABET, 65" x 77"
Zena Thorpe, Chatsworth, CA

716, MY 6TH GRADE SHOES, 70" x 70"
Penelope Tucker & Ronda K. Beyer
San Jose, CA

717, MAMA'S SUNFLOWER GARDEN, 62" x 64"
Charla J. Viehe, Olive Branch, MS

801, RUTH'S QUILT, 74½" x 74½"
Maggie Ball, Bainbridge Island, WA

Mama's Garden by Judy Martin, Quiltmaker, Fall/Winter, 1983

Zebra Fandango by Elizabeth Bren, *Down Under Quilts*, Issue #78, 2004

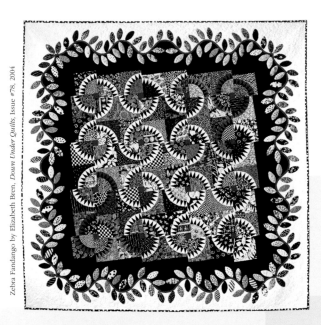

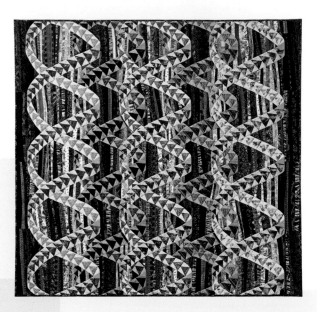

802, On the Wings of a Dream, 72¾" x 72¾"
Ana Buzzalino, Calgary, Alberta, Canada

803, Relationship, 65" x 61"
Jae Eun Cheon, Sungnam,
Gyeonggi-do, South Korea

804, Spectacular, 72¾" x 73"
Joan Davis, Hill City, SD

805, Gear Games, 71" x 71"
Joanne Adams Duncan & Dawna Callahan
Sammamish, WA

Based on the Crossroads quilt by Kazue Takao,
Quilters Newsletter Magazine cover, Nov. 2003

Firm Foundations: Techniques and Quilt Blocks for Precision Piecing by Jane Hall and Dixie Haywood, American Quilter's Society

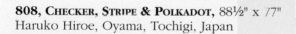
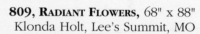

806, FLYWAY, 62" x 62"
Dixie Haywood, Pendleton, SC

807, SEURAT'S DOTS AND ZYDECO, 65" x 81¼"
Dianne S. Hire, Northport, ME

808, CHECKER, STRIPE & POLKADOT, 88½" x 77"
Haruko Hiroe, Oyama, Tochigi, Japan

809, RADIANT FLOWERS, 68" x 88"
Klonda Holt, Lee's Summit, MO

Yoko Ueda class

Radiant Suns pattern by Cara Gulati, Doodle Press

810, Yesterday and Today in Harmony
60" x 59½", Michael Kashey, Edinboro, PA

811, Squash Blossom, 73" x 73"
Georgette Kent, Washington, UT

812, It Takes Time, 72" x 72"
Karen Kielmeyer, Bella Vista, AR

813, Epilogue (I), 76" x 76"
Jung Ran Kim, Seoul, South Korea

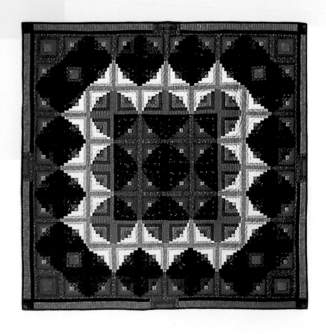

814, Coral Reef, 70" x 70"
Noriko Kobayashi
Keunan-ku, Yokohama, Japan

815, Starting Off, 75¼" x 76½"
Kimiko Kudo, Tokushima, Japan

816, Orient Express, 65½" x 66½"
Elizabeth Lanzatella, Minneapolis, MN

817, Cosmati Stars, 78" x 78"
Judy Mathieson, Sebastopol, CA

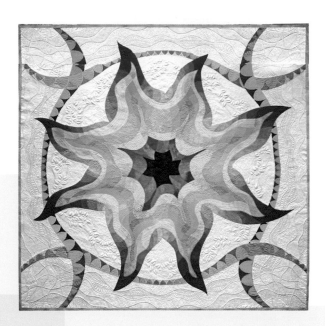

818, PEACH GARDEN, 73" x 78"
Tadako Nagasawa, Nagoya, Aichi, Japan

819, STAR SIGN, 89" x 89"
Philippa Naylor
Beverley, East Yorkshire, England

820, CRYSTAL REVELATION, 72" x 72"
Susan Nelson, Prior Lake, MN

821, TANGERINE, 68" x 68"
Sandra Peterson, Muncie, IN

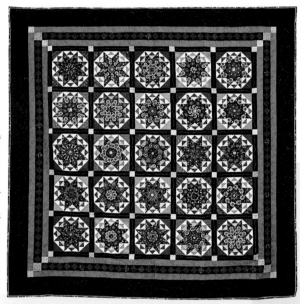

Block pattern from *Pieced Borders: The Complete Resource* by Judy Martin and Marsha McCloskey, Crosley-Griffith Publishing Co.

822, Picanté, 78" x 78"
Nancy Rink, Bakersfield, CA

Mohawk Trail pattern, *Sharp Pointies and Other Paper Pieced Quilts* by Brenda Henning, Bear Paw Productions

823, Rolling Thunder, 76" x 76"
Maria C. Shell & LeAnn McGinnis
Anchorage, AK

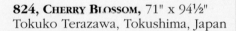

824, Cherry Blossom, 71" x 94½"
Tokuko Terazawa, Tokushima, Japan

825, Luminous Diamonds, 74" x 55"
Cathy Tomm, Leduc, Alberta, Canada

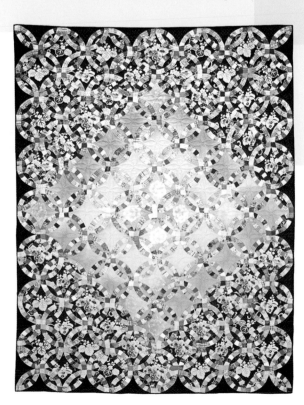

Double Wedding Ring, *A Loving Study of American Patchwork Quilts,* 1983, by Kei Kobayashi; Quilt Square workshop with Kayoko Oguri

Curve Two-Patch, *A Loving Study of American Patchwork Quilts*, 1983, by Kei Kobayashi; Quilt Square workshop with Kayoko Oguri

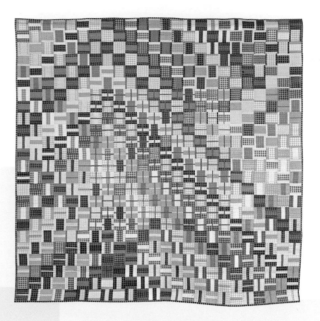

826, AUTUMN IN VILLAGE, 78" x 72½"
Sumako Tukihara, Naka, Tokushima, Japan

827, COMPLETELY DOTTY, 72" x 72"
Kent Williams, Madison, WI

901, NIGHTSHADE, 77" x 78"
Esther Aliu, Melbourne, Victoria, Australia

902, BELLE GOLDA, 81" x 81"
Leanne M. Baraban, Overland Park, KS

Cottage Garden, *Quilting the Garden* by Barb Adams, Alma Allen, and Ricki Creamer, Kansas City Star Books

903, STRING OF PEARLS©, 75" x 84"
Mary S. Buvia, Greenwood, IN

904, ON THE NILE, 62½" x 45½"
Ann Fahl, Racine, WI

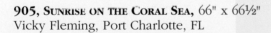

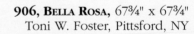

905, SUNRISE ON THE CORAL SEA, 66" x 66½"
Vicky Fleming, Port Charlotte, FL

906, BELLA ROSA, 67¾" x 67¾"
Toni W. Foster, Pittsford, NY

An Unusual Lone Star, *Karen K. Stone Quilts* by Karen K. Stone, Electric Quilt Co.

Rose and Ivy appliqué pattern, Curiosity

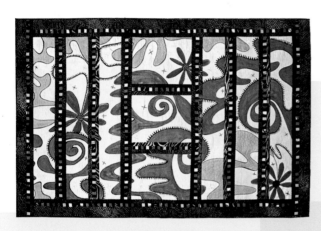

Yoko Ueda class

907, Child's Play: Day Dreams, 78" x 52"
Barbara Oliver Hartman, Flower Mound, TX

908, A Waltz of Circle, 90" x 90"
Haruko Hiroe, Oyama, Tochigi, Japan

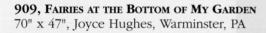

909, Fairies at the Bottom of My Garden
70" x 47", Joyce Hughes, Warminster, PA

910, Indian Summer, 67" x 78"
Jan Hutchison, Sedgwick, KS

Noriko Masui workshop

911, COMBINATION, 60" x 80"
Yuriko Ikuma, Hamamatsu, Shizuoka, Japan

912, THE BIRTH, 73" x 73"
Kiyoko Ishihara, Ashikaga, Tochigi, Japan

913, SYLVAN SPLASH, 65" x 62"
Susan Jackan, Madison, WI

914, SOUND OF SOUL, 85" x 85"
Sachiko Kawamitsu, Amstelveen, Netherlands

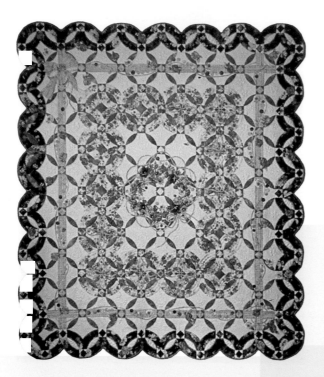

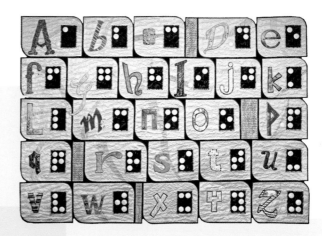

915, The 25th Wedding Anniversary
66" x 76", Yoshiko Kitami
Inabe, Mie, Japan

916, The Gift of Sight, 73" x 51"
Pat LaPierre, Bass Harbor, ME

917, Let Your Light Shine, 82" x 82"
Linda MacDougall, Murrieta, CA

918, Exuberance, 77½" x 77½"
Margaret McDonald
Lockwood South, Victoria, Australia

919, COOL CAMELS OF EGYPT, 70" x 54½"
Barbara Barrick McKie, Lyme, CT

920, THE GARDEN OF THE SANCTUARY, 75" x 82"
Hiroko Nakamura
Shimajiri, Okinawa, Japan

921, HEART QUILT, 72½" x 72½"
Judy O'Connell, North Richland Hills, TX

922, REQUIEM (BLUE LEAVES GARDEN), 77" x 77"
Mikiko Ogura, Hachioji, Tokyo, Japan

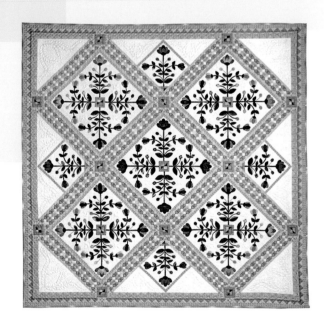

Heart Quilt, Vintage Valentine by Verna Mosquera of The Vintage Spool

Based on African art by E. Gamma from South Africa

923, African Curves, 68" x 71"
Sonja Ohlmann, Leduc, Alberta, Canada

924, Sweet Land of Liberty, 79" x 79"
Marlene Tamm Royse, Raleigh, NC

925, Fan-Crested Magenticus, 68½" x 68"
Janet Simmons Scheer, Corpus Christi, TX

926, Contemporary Fruit Salad, 62" x 62"
Mary Tabar, San Diego, CA

Workshop with Darlene Christopherson

927, MIDNIGHT ROSE, 73½" x 73½"
Kazue Takao, Utsunomiya, Tochigi, Japan

928, FOLIAGE IN TRANSITION, 79½" x 59½"
Carol Taylor, Pittsford, NY

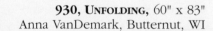

929, EARLY SPRING SONG, 76" x 76"
Etsuko Uto, Kashima, Ibaraki, Japan

930, UNFOLDING, 60" x 83"
Anna VanDemark, Butternut, WI

Great Book of Celtic Patterns by Lora S. Irish, Fox Chapel Publishing; seminar and online videos by Ricky Tims; *The Grammar of Ornament: All 100 Color Plates from the Folio Edition of the Great Victorian Sourcebook of Historic Design* by Owen Jones, Dover Publications

931, TWIST, 62" x 62"
Elsie Vredenburg, Tustin, MI

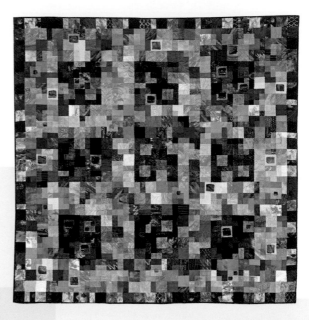

932, SQUARED UP, 80" x 80"
Lisa Walton & Nic Bridges
Sydney, NSW, Australia

933, GRANDMA JEANNE'S COUNTRY ALBUM QUILT
68" x 68", Jeanne Whaley, Oscoda, MI

934, CROSSROAD, 78" x 78"
Kyoko Yano, Sayama, Saitama, Japan

Grandma's Country Album pattern by Robert Callaham, *McCall's Quilting*, 1998–1999 1010. Prismatic Flowers workshop, Barbara Olson, Barbara Olson Designs (6 issues)

935, Chanticleer, 60½" x 60½"
Marla Yeager, Ava, MO

1001, The Zodiac, 90" x 90"
Martha Brown, Pickering, Ontario, Canada

1002, Little Piece of Heaven, 68" x 90"
Mary S. Buvia, Greenwood, IN

1003, Panthera Tigris, 64" x 42"
Janneke De Vries Bodzinga
Kollumerzwaag, Netherlands

1004, SUMMER MNEMONIC, 60" x 63"
Barbara Hendrick Dorn, Canton, GA

1005, AFRICA, THE LION LURKS, 98" x 98"
Linda Hibbert, Loveland, CO

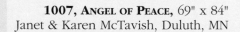

1006, SPECTATORS, 66" x 68"
Inge Mardal & Steen Hougs, Chantilly, France

1007, ANGEL OF PEACE, 69" x 84"
Janet & Karen McTavish, Duluth, MN

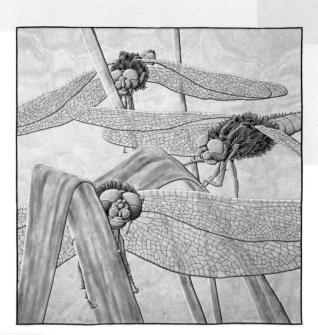

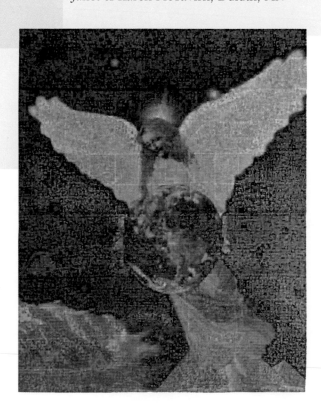

1009, LAZY AFTERNOON, 64¼" x 47"
Ruth Powers, Carbondale, KS

1010, LAS FLORES, 65" x 95"
Pat Rollie, Los Angeles, CA

1011, ECHOES, 63" x 40"
Carol Seeley, Campbell River,
British Columbia, Canada

*Quilting—it's a hobby that
can last a lifetime.*

BONNIE K. BROWNING

1012, Chance Encounter, 88" x 75"
Rita Steffenson, Urbana, OH

1013, Indian Woman, 64" x 86"
Stacy Tambornino, Chippewa Falls, WI

1014, Match the Bears, 70" x 81"
Cathy Wiggins, Macon, NC

1101, Vital Energies, 57" x 85"
Tomoko Arai
Tsuruoka, Yamagata, Japan

Earthdancer cross-stitch pattern by Marilyn Leavitt-Imblum

5,500 Quilt Block Designs by Maggie Malone, Sterling Publishing

1102, ANTIQUE FLOWERS, 48½" x 52½"
Betty Cabe, Franklin, NC

Center based on Paula Nadelstern's Kaleidoscope technique

1103, SAMARKAND, 42" x 41"
Sandy Curran, Newport News, VA

1104, SUNSHINE SURFING, 53" x 53"
Emanuela D'Amico, Rome, Italy

1105, COSMIC KALEIDOSCOPE II, 42¼" x 42¼"
Barbara Dowdy-Trabke & Angela Klueppel,
Reno, NV

Space Crystal 2 pattern, *Big Book of Building Block Quilts* by Sara Nephew,
Clearview Triangle

Carnival Beauty, Radiant New York Beauties: 14 Paper-Pieced Quilt Projects by Valori Wells, C&T Publishing, Inc.

1106, BEAUTY-FULL SUNRISE, 40" x 44"
Susie Dumas, Macon, GA

1107, MY STASH AT 50, 42" x 50"
Karen Eckmeier, Kent, CT

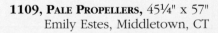

1108, LEAVES, LEAVES & MORE LEAVES
46" x 46", Carole Elsbree, Sunriver, OR

1109, PALE PROPELLERS, 45¼" x 57"
Emily Estes, Middletown, CT

Happy2/Joy2 pattern by Patricia Hess, Quilters Newsletter Magazine, June 2001

Propeller blocks from Confetti Quilts: A No-Fuss Approach to Color, Fabric & Design by Mary Mashuta, C&T Publishing

Love Apple Star, *Flowering Favorites from Piece O' Cake Designs* by Becky Goldsmith & Linda Jenkins, C&T Publishing, Inc.; Cottage Garden, *Quilting the Garden* by Barb Adams, Alma Allen, and Ricki Creamer, Kansas City Star Books; selected flowers from Blackbird Designs

Inspired by *The Romance of the Patchwork Quilt in America* by Carrie A. Hall and Rose Kretsinger, Bonanza Books

1110, ROCKY MOUNTAIN FLORAL BOUQUET
41" x 41", Sandi Fruehling, Aurora, CO

1111, OLLIE JANE'S FLOWER GARDEN
58½" x 68", Sandra Gilreath, Bonaire, GA

1112, MOUNTAIN STAR, 43" x 41½"
Lynne G. Harrill, Greenville, SC

1113, A TRELLISED ARBOUR, 58½" x 58½"
Dawn S. Hayes, Upper Montclair, NJ

Distinctive Pieces patterns by Susan R. DuLaney, www.DistinctivePieces.com

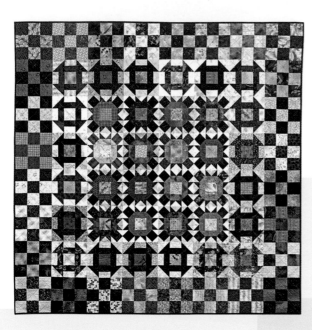

1114, Nine Patch Jazz, 59" x 59"
Wendy Hill, Sunriver, OR

1115, Topsy Turvy Nine Patch, 59" x 76"
Judy Laquidara, Nevada, MO

1116, Happy Moments, 57" x 57"
Hila Leslie,
Niteroi, Rio de Janeiro, Brazil

1117, Not Your Mother's Scraps, 53" x 53"
Elaine Letz & Leanne Spencer, Copley, OH

Topsy Turvy Nine-Patch pattern by Judy Laquidara, American Quilter, Projects Issue 2007

The Colourful Quilt pattern by Jacqueline de Jonge, Becolourful, www.becolourful.com

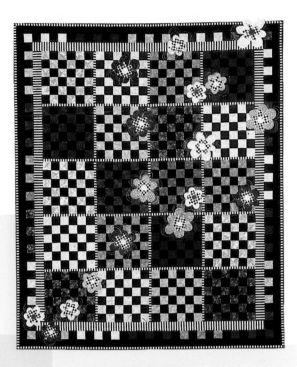

1118, PRINCESS FEATHERS AND COCKSCOMBS
57" x 57", Rhoda Libiez, Canton, OH

1119, FLOWER POWER, 53" x 64"
Janice Maddox, Asheville, NC

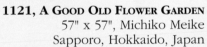

1120, STAR LIGHT, STAR BRIGHT, 47" x 58"
Charlotte McRanie, Marietta, GA

1121, A GOOD OLD FLOWER GARDEN
57" x 57", Michiko Meike
Sapporo, Hokkaido, Japan

Curvaceous Squares workshop with Dianne Hire

Stars in the Night Sky, *A New Turn on Drunkard's Path* by Mary Sue Suit, Martingale & Company, Inc.

1122, Did I Do That? 44" x 53"
Nancy Peters, Wildwood, MO

1123, African Nights, 40" x 48"
Helen Roemisch, West Columbia, TX

1124, Star of the Serengeti, 48½" x 49"
Tess Thorsberg, Macon, GA

1125, To the Heaven, 52" x 68½"
Akiko Torii, Aizumi, Tokushima, Japan

Inspired by Black and Checkers quilt by Viola Colombe, *Quilters Newsletter Magazine,* April 2007

Mariner's Compass, *A Loving Study of American Patchwork Quilts,* 1983, by Kei Kobayashi; Quilt Square workshop with Kayoko Oguri

1126, COZY CABIN ROSE, 58½" x 58½"
Sue Turnquist, Oakdale, CT

1127, FINALLY FEATHERED, 45" x 41"
Marla Head Whalen, Arlington, TN

1128, BOREALIS, 52" x 52½"
Marla Yeager, Ava, MO

1129, OH, MY STARS! 55" x 55"
Glennes M. Youngbauer
Boulder Junction, WI

The Unnamed Star, *The It's Okay If You Sit On My Quilt Book* by Mary Ellen Hopkins, C&T Publishing, Inc.

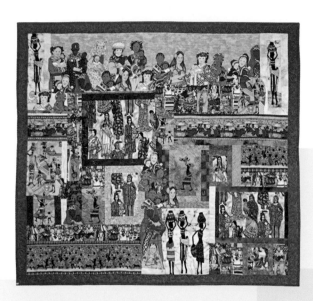

1201, MOTHERS AND CHILDREN, 47" x 42½"
Marina Baudoin, Silver Spring, MD

1202, STARBURST, 52" x 52"
Irena Bluhm, Antlers, OK

1203, SOUL MATES, 58" x 72"
Eun Ryoung Choi
Seocho-Gu, Seoul, South Korea

1204, SUNSHINE BRIGHT CIRCLE PLAY
41" x 47", Dot Collins, Port Neches, TX

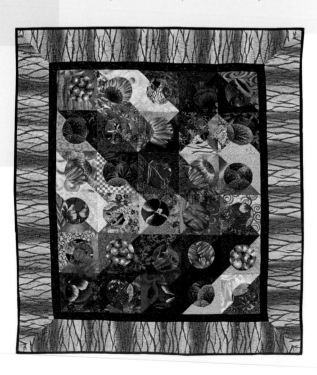

Circle Play workshop with Reynola Pakusich

1205, A Unique Perspective, 41½" x 49"
Amy Cunningham-Waltz, Waltham, MA

1206, The Ninepatchers • The Scrappy Family,
49" x 53", Mickey Depre, Oak Lawn, IL

1207, Under the Rainbow, 41½" x 57½"
Diane Rusin Doran, Glenelg, MD

1208, Remembering Barbaro, 44" x 59"
Sheril Drummond, Lexington, KY

1209, WHISPERS OF HOPE, 52" x 44"
Pat Durbin, Eureka, CA

1210, GROOVY GUITARS TOO! 40" x 55"
Robbi Joy Eklow, Third Lake, IL

1211, GLOBAL WARMING, 49¾" x 61½"
Anna Faustino, North Arlington, NJ

1212, STARS OVER PADUCAH, 51" x 65"
Donna Gabbard, Cincinnati, OH

Woven Stars workshop with Sally Schneider

1213, A GLIMPSE OF TUSCANY, 41½" x 51"
Sherrie Grob, Murphysboro, IL

1214, ANIMALS OF AUSTRALIA IN THE OLGAS LANDSCAPE, 51" x 74", Julie Haddrick
Blackwood, Adelaide, South Australia

1215, BLUSHING TRIANGLES 3, 41½" x 42"
Gloria Hansen, East Windsor, NJ

1216, SHRINE, 58" x 77"
Barbara Oliver Hartman
Flower Mound, TX

Workshop with Rami Kim

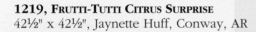

1217, Sewing Time, 43" x 45", Oh Sun Hee
Yongin, Gyeonggi-do, South Korea

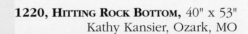

1218, Sunflower, 43" x 40"
Charlotte Hickman, Oklahoma City, OK

1219, Frutti-Tutti Citrus Surprise
42½" x 42½", Jaynette Huff, Conway, AR

1220, Hitting Rock Bottom, 40" x 53"
Kathy Kansier, Ozark, MO

Appliqué leaf design by Gwen Marston

1221, PRAYING TREE, 47" x 59"
Joung Soon Kim, Daegu, South Korea

1222, HALLOWEEN HAUNTS, 52½" x 71"
Nadine K. Kirk, Torrance, CA

1223, PSALM 46:10 BE STILL, 40¼" x 40¼"
Suzanne Kistler, Visalia, CA

1224, THE SUN IN SPLENDOR, 55" x 55"
Chris Kleppe, Milwaukee, WI

1225, Sol Play, 59" x 48"
Pat Kroth, Verona, WI

1226, Leaf in Transition, 44" x 51½"
Marilyn League, Memphis, TN

1227, Garden, 58" x 58"
Jung Sun Lee, Seoul, South Korea

1228, Glimmer in the Forest, 40" x 55"
Janice Maddox, Asheville, NC

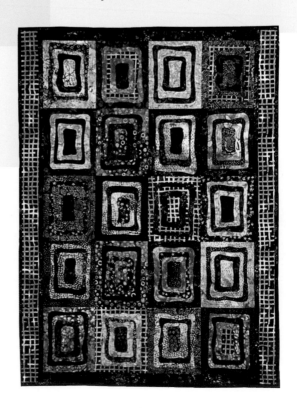

1229, BANYAN TREES, 60" x 40"
Joyce Martelli, Rochester, NY

1230, PLAYING IN THE PARK, 41½" x 47½"
Nancy Sterett Martin, Owensboro, KY

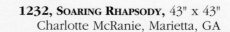

1231, AFTERNOON SEDUCTION, 43½" x 46½"
Barbara Barrick McKie, Lyme, CT

1232, SOARING RHAPSODY, 43" x 43"
Charlotte McRanie, Marietta, GA

Class with Ricky Tims

1233, ORCHID STUDY II, 43" x 62"
Stephanie Nordlin, Poplar Grove, IL

1234, JUST ANOTHER LOG CABIN QUILT
51" x 42", Charles O'Kelley
Tuscaloosa, AL

1235, VIBRATION OF INDIGO BLUE, 51¼" x 67"
Kayoko Oguri, Kaifu, Tokushima, Japan

1236, FOXFIRES, 52¾" x 57¾"
Frieda Oxenham, West Linton,
Peeblesshire, United Kingdom

1237, THE SILVERY WAVES, 45" x 40"
Young Yai Park, Yongin,
Gyeonggi-do, South Korea

1238, GOLDEN GLOW, 59½" x 59½"
Elaine Plogman, Cincinnati, OH

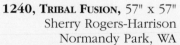

1239, THE SKY IS FALLING, 49½" x 62½"
Linda Reinert, Oregon City, OR

1240, TRIBAL FUSION, 57" x 57"
Sherry Rogers-Harrison
Normandy Park, WA

Twisted Bargello pattern by Chris Timmins, Australia

Fantastic Fabric Folding: Innovative Quilting Projects by Rebecca Wat,
C&T Publishing

1241, IMPERIAL HOUSE OF KOI, 45" x 52½"
Maurine Roy, Edmonds, WA

1242, FLOWERS, FROGS, AND FISHES
44½" x 47", Mary C. Schroeder
North Bend, OR

1243, FALL INTO SPRING, 55½" x 55½"
Cheryl L. See, Ashburn, VA

1244, HYPNOTIC HYPOTENUSE, 50" x 60"
Maria C. Shell, Anchorage, AK

*The Crafter's Pattern Sourcebook by Mary MacCarthy, pages 28 & 137, Trafalgar
Square Publishing; Leaf patterns, 505 Quilt Blocks: Plus 36 Beautiful Projects to
Make, Better Homes & Gardens*

**1245, GRANDMOTHER'S PSYCHEDELIC
FLOWER GARDEN,** 44" x 56"
Barbara Shiffler, Statesboro, GA

1246, DECIPHER, 42½" x 55½"
Carol Taylor, Pittsford, NY

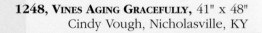

1247, DAISY CHAIN, 50½" x 50½"
Camille Vlasak, Collierville, TN

1248, VINES AGING GRACEFULLY, 41" x 48"
Cindy Vough, Nicholasville, KY

Rhapsody Quilts workshop with Ricky Tims

1249, A Touch of Red, 42" x 42"
Marilyn H. Wall & Diana Pickens
West Union, SC

1250, Orchidaceous, 47" x 47"
Rachel A. Wetzler, St. Charles, IL

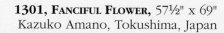

1251, Two-Thirds Majority, 40" x 50"
Kent Williams, Madison, WI

1301, Fanciful Flower, 57½" x 69"
Kazuko Amano, Tokushima, Japan

Quilt Square workshop with Kayoko Oguri

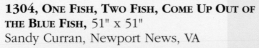

1302, GORILLA GORILLA, 56" x 47"
Nancy S. Brown, Oakland, CA

1303, HELP! THERE'S A CHICKEN IN MY CHILI
43½" x 43½", Sheri Mears Cooper
Winchester, MA

1304, ONE FISH, TWO FISH, COME UP OUT OF THE BLUE FISH, 51" x 51"
Sandy Curran, Newport News, VA

1305, AUTUMN IN GOD'S COUNTRY, 42" x 45"
Barbara Daniel, Ducor, CA

PHOTOGRAPH NOT AVAILABLE

1306, SAWTOOTH DRAGON, 53" x 53"
Jean L. DellaMonica, Calabasas, CA

1307, AFRICAN PRINCESS, 57" x 70"
Diane M. DiMaria, Santa Fe, NM

1308, FOR THESE WOODS, 41" x 46"
Rebecca Douglas, Punta Gorda, FL

1309, CALIFORNIA GOLD, 57" x 45"
Pat Durbin, Eureka, CA

"A Blessing for the Woods," poem by Michael S. Glaser, used with permission

Inspired by image in *Traditional Chinese Textile Designs in Full Color,* page 32, edited by the Northeast Drama Institute, Dover Publications

1310, THE BODACIOUS DINER©, 40" x 41"
Margie Engel, Satellite Beach, FL

1311, PHOENIX AND FLORA, 40" x 42¾"
Margaret Ferguson
Glace Bay, Nova Scotia, Canada

1312, FILLYAW FOREST, 42" x 74"
Mary Ann Fielder, Manchester, MI

1313, A PICTURE FROM ITALY, 40" x 49"
Cathy Geier, Waukesha, WI

1314, Four Seasons, 55" x 44"
Diane Getty, Baltimore, MD

1315, Souvenir of Florence, 53" x 41"
Carol Goddu, Mississauga, Ontario, Canada

1316, Magnus Hall, 53" x 45¼"
Leslie A. Hall, Longboat Key, FL

1317, Baghdad Burning, 44½" x 53"
Donna Hussain, Sacramento, CA

1318, John in Sunshine and Shadow, 52" x 52"
Deborah Hyde, West Bloomfield, MI

1319, Rose Garden, 40" x 50"
Joung Soon Kim, Daegu, South Korea

1320, The Estate Sale, 46" x 41"
Dort Lee, Leicester, NC

1321, Libellula Saturata, Flame Skimmer,
54" x 42", Tonya Littmann, Denton, TX

Inspired by old Swiss tapestries, circa 1430

1322, We're Not in Kansas Anymore, II,
58½" x 67", Karlyn Bue Lohrenz, Billings, MT

1323, The Beast and His Boy, 56" x 43"
Suzanne Marshall, Clayton, MO

1324, Much Ado About Nothing, 57" x 43"
Kathy McNeil, Tulalip, WA

1325, En Garde, 45" x 72"
Roberta Reskusich, Glen Carbon, IL

Dragonslayer, *Once upon a Quilt: Fairy Tales in Fabric* by Bonnie Kaster and Virginia Athey, Martingale & Company, Inc.

Quilt Square workshop with Kayoko Oguri

1326, THREE WOMEN OF JAIPUR, 49" x 81"
Ruthanne Rocha, Miranda, CA

1327, THE SUMMER BREEZE, 54¼" x 71½"
Hideko Ryuki, Tokushima, Japan

1328, MOOSE DROOL, 57" x 44"
Carla Selberg, Brunswick, ME

1329, WINTER ENCOUNTER, 54" x 46½"
Carol Ann Sinnreich, Lawton, OK

Based on a photo by Stan Legure

Workshop with Katie Pasquini Masopust

1330, PETRIFIED FOREST, 41" x 65"
Brenda H. Smith, Flagstaff, AZ

1331, KOI, 41" x 57"
Sarah Ann Smith, Camden, ME

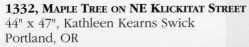

1332, MAPLE TREE ON NE KLICKITAT STREET
44" x 47", Kathleen Kearns Swick
Portland, OR

1333, SALLY AT THE WINDOW, 40" x 51"
David M. Taylor, Steamboat Springs, CO

Workshop with Ruth McDowell

Adapted from a photo by Ken Proper, The Proper Exposure

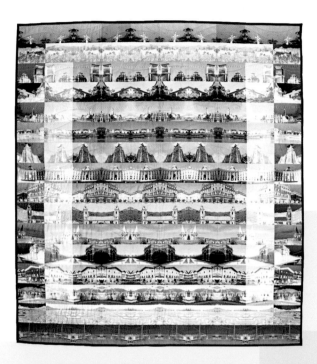

1334, Danube Drifting, 47" x 53"
Judy Mercer Tescher, Pendleton, IN

1335, Yellow Chair Loves Apples, 42" x 44"
Laura Wasilowski, Elgin, IL

1336, Delicious, 56½" x 64"
Rachel Wetzler, St. Charles, IL

1337, Pearsall Gate: Entering Eternity
46" x 47", Mary Wilber Wirchansky
Schenevus, NY

Enchanted Views: Quilts Inspired by Wrought-Iron Designs by Dilys A. Fronks, C&T Publishing, Inc.; Casting Shadows: Creating Visual Dimension in Your Quilts by Colleen Wise, C&T Publishing, Inc.

1338, Beauty Pageant, 49" x 48½"
Marlene Brown Woodfield, LaPorte, IN

1339, Nature of Korea, 55" x 65"
Kim Yoonkyoung
DoBong Gu, Seoul, South Korea

1401, Stream of Consciousness
48½" x 45½", Lashonne Abel, Birmingham, AL

1402, Jack & Jill, 47½" x 47½"
Barbara Aldeman, Schaumburg, IL

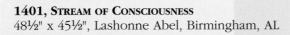

Head for the Borders Workshop with Barb Vlack; Aunt Martha's Hot Iron Transfers, Colonial Patterns, Inc.

Hummingbird design from Embroidery Library, Inc., www.emblibrary.com

1403, A MATTER OF TIME, 58" x 42"
Judy Alexander, Marietta, GA

1404, FLORENCE AND BERNICE TAKE A STROLL
47" x 59½", Jody Aultman, Hugo, MN

1405, LIFE'S DELICATE JOURNEY, 43" x 40"
Deborah Baldwin, Oak Park, IL

1406, ROMAN PATIENCE, 57" x 55"
Dena Bauer, Wadesville, IN

Perspective, Quilt University Online Class with Susan Brittingham

Zig and Zag pattern by Linda Hibbert, Silver Linings Originals

1407, Some Things ARE Black and White
58" x 54", Carol S. Carter, Marshfield, WI

1408, The Revery Alone Will Do, 40" x 40"
Daniela Cassani, Varese, Italy

1409, Mystique, 53½" x 55"
Sue Chaffee, Overland Park, KS

1410, Grand Canyon Monarch, 42" x 63"
Donna Cherry, Bend, OR

Design class with Karen McTavish

1411, WHEN YOU WISH, 43" x 43"
Sheri Mears Cooper, Winchester, MA

1412, WILDFLOWERS AND WEEDS, 60" x 60"
Rebecca Douglas, Punta Gorda, FL

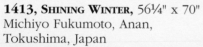

1413, SHINING WINTER, 56¼" x 70"
Michiyo Fukumoto, Anan,
Tokushima, Japan

1414, WOODLAND CREATURES, 58" x 78"
Ingrid Fullard, Georgetown, TX

Quilt Square workshop with Kayoko Oguri

Woodland Creatures patterns by Rosemary Makhan

Heart Sampler Quilt. *Appliqué! Appliqué!! Appliqué!!! The Complete Guide to Hand Appliqué* by Laurene Sinema, The Quilt Digest Press

1415, MEXICAN FLOWER BOWLS, 42" x 42"
Sylvia Gegaregian, Portola Valley, CA

1416, A CHANGE OF HEART, 46" x 46½"
Victoria Gray, Heffley Creek,
British Columbia, Canada

1417, KALEIDOSCOPE, 41½" x 41½"
Sachiko Hanano, Okayama, Japan

1418, CYCLING SPOKES, 52" x 52"
Bill Horst, Winnetka, CA

Nelson's Victory, *A Loving Study of American Patchwork Quilts, 1983,* by Kei Kobayashi; Quilt Square workshop with Kayoko Oguri

Brilliance pattern, Jinny Beyer's Mystery Quilt by Jinny Beyer, *McCall's Quilting,* October 2007

Daisies Do Tell, *Follow The Dots to Dazzling Quilts* by Joan Segna and Jayme Crow, That Patchwork Place

Curve Two Patch, *A Loving Study of American Patchwork Quilts*, 1983, by Kei Kobayashi; Quilt Square workshop with Kayoko Oguri

1419, PLEASE DON'T PICK THE DAISIES
49½" x 70", Ann Jones, Poulsbo, WA

1420, IN THE FAR DISTANCE, 57¾" x 70"
Michiko Kohashi, Tokushima, Japan

1421, GRACE, 49¼" x 49¾"
Vicki Krohn, Mantua, OH

1422, WE'RE NOT IN KS ANYMORE
44½" x 46½", Dottie Lankard
Independence, KS

RaNae Merrill spirals class

The Colourful Quilt pattern by Jacqueline de Jonge, Be-Colourful

1423, BOURBON STREET, 52" x 52"
Elizabeth Lanzatella, Minneapolis, MN

1424, GARDEN GROOVE, 40" x 40"
Linda MacDougall, Murrieta, CA

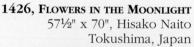

1425, SPRING TIME WANDERING, 47" x 40"
Calna McGoldrick, Echo Bay, Ontario, Canada

1426, FLOWERS IN THE MOONLIGHT
57½" x 70", Hisako Naito
Tokushima, Japan

Sunburst Magic by Yoshihiro Amano, Patchwork Pattern 1000, 2004;
Quilt Square workshop with Kayoko Oguri

1427, Grandma's Clock, 55" x 55"
Jodi Robinson, Enon Valley, PA

Leaves, Art Glass Quilts: New Subtractive Appliqué Technique by Julie Hirota,
C&T Publishing

1428, My Neon Leaves, 48" x 52"
Karen Smalley, Lexington, KY

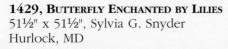

1429, Butterfly Enchanted by Lilies
51½" x 51½", Sylvia G. Snyder
Hurlock, MD

1430, Lingering Doodle, 40" x 41"
Stephanie Sprinkle, Miamisburg, OH

1431, Sunflowers and Cabbage Whites
46" x 86", Lauren Strach, St Joseph, MI

1432, Garden Path, 49" x 65"
Priscilla Stultz, Fairfax, VA

1433, A Journey to Light, 47" x 51"
Stacy Tambornino, Chippewa Falls, WI

1434, KT-22 in Cloth, 46" x 46"
B. Lynn Tubbe, Georgetown, CA

A Journey to Light by McKenna Ryan, Pine Needles Designs

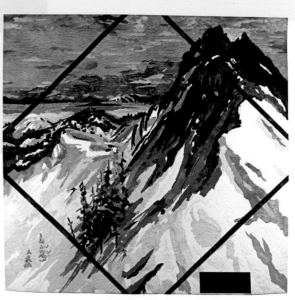

Squaw Valley's KT-22 by Cecile Johnson, watercolor adapted with permission

1435, WINDOW ON THE WORLD, 41" x 42"
Sharon Wasteney, Ellston, IA

1436, SLICE OF FLORIDA, 40" x 47"
Candace West, Floral City, FL

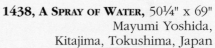

1437, HOMAGE, 49" x 49"
Christine M. Wickert, Penfield, NY

1438, A SPRAY OF WATER, 50¼" x 69"
Mayumi Yoshida,
Kitajima, Tokushima, Japan

Working on the Edge workshop with Sally Collins; Compass Rose pattern, *Quiltmaking by Hand: Simple Stitches, Exquisite Quilts* by Jinny Beyer, Breckling Press; *4" Sampler-Book 1: Includes 225 Different Blocks* by Jill Kemp, Bear Paw Designs; *Medallion Quilts: Inspiration & Patterns* by Cindy Vermillion Hamilton, American Quilter's Society

Barbara Bannister Star, *A Loving Study of American Patchwork Quilts* by Kei Kobayashi; Quilt Square workshop with Kayoko Oguri

1501, One Tree Quilt, 42" x 64"
Naomi S. Adams, Round Rock, TX

1502, Spirals, 75" x 88"
Tara Faughnan, Oakland, CA

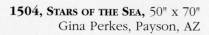

1503, Rachel's Quilt, 82" x 96"
Heidi K. Meyer, Richland Center, WI

1504, Stars of the Sea, 50" x 70"
Gina Perkes, Payson, AZ

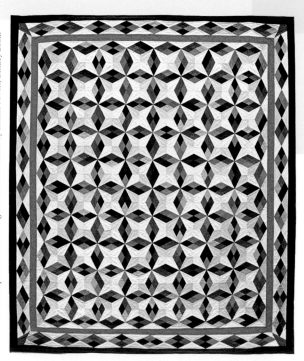

Pattern adapted from cover design of *Arkansas Traveler* by Earlene Fowler, Berkley Books

1505, SEVEN LITTLE PIGLETS QUILTING WORKSHOP
59" x 51½", Namiji Suarez, Orlando, FL

1506, TOUR EIFFEL, 41⅞" x 51½"
Ann Wasserburger, Laramie, WY

1507, ENCOMPASSING ORANGE, 54" x 54"
Susan Webster, Apple Valley, MN

Medallion class with Gwen Lundgren

*The world is but a canvas
to the imagination.*

HENRY DAVID THOREAU

Elements in Fabric Quilt University workshop with Linda Schmidt

1601, DAYDREAMING, 17½" x 17"
Judy Alexander, Marietta, GA

1602, WIND IN THE WILLOWS, 12" x 12"
Mary Arnold, Vancouver, WA

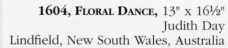

1603, MORE CARROTS, PLEASE, 16" x 16"
Jean Biddick, Tucson, AZ

1604, FLORAL DANCE, 13" x 16½"
Judith Day
Lindfield, New South Wales, Australia

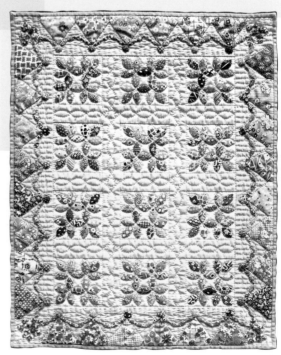

Photo adaptation from *Gathered in Time: Utah Quilts* by Kae Covington, University of Utah Press

Traditional 7's Block, EQ5 Software

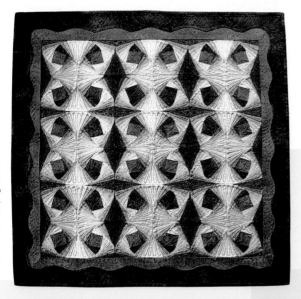

1605, EARTHEN WAVES, 16½" x 16½"
Leigh Elking, Scottsdale, AZ

1606, LOG CABIN, 17¼" x 17¼"
Sherry Fourez, Saint Joseph, IL

1607, CELESTIAL GARDEN, 16" x 16"
Jane Holihan, Walworth, NY

1608, PALAMPORE, 11" x 13¼"
Pat Holly, Ann Arbor, MI

Inspired by an 1800 crewel embroidery

1609, ANTIQUE CHINA CABINET, 18¼" x 22"
Jaynette Huff, Conway, AR

1610, SPRING PASTORALE, 21⅞" x 23¼"
Jan Hutchison, Sedgwick, KS

1611, CHARLESTON REVISITED, 22½" x 22½"
Patricia Krohn, Raleigh, NC

1612, SOLITAIRE, 15" x 15"
Pat Kuhns, Lincoln, NE

Workshop with Noriko Shimano

Safe Harbor by Pat Kuhns, *Blue Ribbon Miniature Quilts*, Chitra Publications

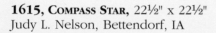

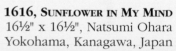

1613, BLOOMS, 22⅞" x 22⅞"
Terumi Kurata, Kumagaya, Saitama, Japan

1614, NORTH AND SOUTH, 16¼" x 16¼"
Vicki Littel, Menomonee Falls, WI

1615, COMPASS STAR, 22½" x 22½"
Judy L. Nelson, Bettendorf, IA

1616, SUNFLOWER IN MY MIND
16½" x 16½", Natsumi Ohara
Yokohama, Kanagawa, Japan

Diamond Jubilee projects, designed by Liz Schwartz and Stephen Seifert; published in *Quilts with Style*, 2006, issues 56–61; www.quiltswithstyle.com

Star of Bethlehem pattern, *Folk Quilts and How to Recreate Them* by Audrey and Douglas Wiss, Sterling Publishing

Pineapple block by Alan Taylor, www.alanandmike.com/miniblocks/

1617, STAR OF BETHLEHEM, 15½" x 15½"
Lorraine Olsen, Springfield, MO

1618, PEACEFUL CHAOS, 13" x 19"
Lori Olson, Brookings, SD

1619, SCRAPMANIA ELEGANTE, A CRAZY QUILT
15" x 15", Roberta Reskusich, Glen Carbon, IL

1620, DANCING RIBBONS, 12" x 12"
Cindy Rounds Richards, Snellville, GA

Motifs for Crazy Quilting: Techniques for Embroidering and Embellishing Crazy Quilts by J. Marsha Michler, Krause Publications

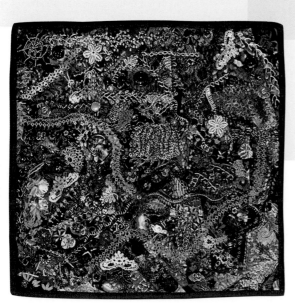

Inspired by photos of antique inlaid tables

Noriko Simano workshop

1621, CARNIVALE, 16" x 16"
Karen Roberts, Cedarburg, WI

1622, SUNNY GARDEN, 22½" x 22½"
Miyoko Shoda
Kumagaya, Saitama, Japan

1623, ILLUSIONS, 11" x 11"
George Siciliano, Lebanon, PA

1624, CONUNDRUM, 19" x 19"
Judy Spiers, Foxworth, MS

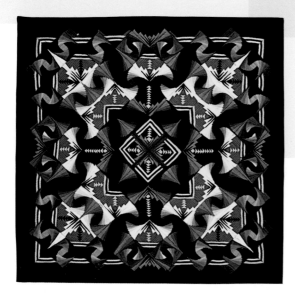

1625, Pixie Stars, 14¼" x 14½"
Patricia L. Styring, St Augustine, FL

1626, On the Green Grass, 12" x 12"
Mie Totsu, Nagano City, Nagano, Japan

1627, Rhapsody in Red, 21¾" x 21¼"
Trudy Søndrol Wasson, Eden Prairie, MN

1628, But Not Forgotten, 20½" x 20½"
Marla Head Whalen, Arlington, TN

Old-Fashioned Floral Designs, #063, Dover Publications

Make your plans to attend now!

Quilt Contest Rules – Paducah

1. The maker of a cloth quilt can enter a completed quilt by submitting entry blank, entry fee, and images of the completed work.

2. Limit of two entries per entrant(s) or group, one entry per category. A group entry (category 5) constitutes one entry for each individual in the group. Those listed as "other stitchers on this quilt" may also have their own two entries.

3. Quilt must be constructed and quilted by person(s) named on entry blank.

4. Quilts stitched by one or two persons can be entered in all categories except 5. Quilts stitched by three or more people can only be entered in Group Category 5.

5. All quilts must be quilted by hand, by machine, or both.

6. Quilt must have been finished between January 1, 2007, and January 1, 2009, and be in excellent condition.

7. Quilts displayed in any previous AQS contests (Paducah, Nashville, or Des Moines), or quilts made from precut or stamped kits are ineligible.

8. Quilts must be a single unit and not framed with wood, metal, etc.

9. Quilts in categories 4 and 14 must be a first-time entry for any stitchers on the quilt in any AQS contest (Paducah, Nashville, or Des Moines).

10. Quilt Sizes: (Actual quilt size must fit dimensions listed for category. All quilts must have the rod pocket sewn ½" from the top edge for hanging. For more information on the new sleeve requirements, see Sleeve Info at www.AmericanQuilter.com under Shows & Contests. A label identifying the maker must be stitched or securely attached to the back lower edge of each quilt.

    a. Bed-sized quilts in categories 1 – 5 must be 60" to 110" in width and a length of 80" or more.

    b. Handmade quilts in category 6 must be 60" to 110" in width and a length of 80" or more.

    c. Large wall quilts, categories 7 – 10, must be 60" to 110" in width and a length of 40" or more.

    d. Small wall quilts, categories 11 – 14, must be 40" to 60" in width and a length of 40" or more.

    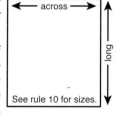

    e. Young Designer quilts in category 15 must be a minimum of 40" or more in width and a length of 40" or more. Quilts can use any traditional or original design elements in a unique interpretation. Young designers must be 18 to 35 years of age (determined on opening date of show).

    f. Miniature quilts in category 16 must be a maximum of 24" in width and length. Sleeves are not needed on miniature quilts.

11. Quilt entries in categories 1–10 will be considered for the AQS Best of Show, AQS Hand Workmanship, Bernina Machine Workmanship, and Gammill Longarm Machine Quilting purchase awards. Quilts in categories 11–14 are eligible for the Moda Best Wall Quilt purchase award. Quilts in category 16 are eligible for the Benartex Best Miniature purchase award. These purchase awards will become a part of the permanent collection of the Museum of the American Quilter's Society. Winners not wishing to relinquish their quilts may retain possession by refusing their prize money. Photography and printing rights must still be granted to AQS. Quilts in category 15 are eligible for the Olfa Young Designer Okada Award.

12. Quilt must be available for judging and display from April 6 through April 28, 2009.

13. Incomplete, torn, or soiled quilts will not qualify for entry or exhibition.

14. Full-view digital photo must show all edges of the finished quilt. Detail photo must show the quilting stitches. Do not send slides.

15. All decisions of the jurors and judges are final. AQS reserves the right to reject any entry, including those that fail to follow the quilt contest rules.

16. Please include the complete name and address of your local newspaper s[...] news release can be sent there.

17. See Categories for descriptions of each category.

18. Semifinalists may sell their quilts at the show. Additional information w[...] be sent with the acceptance letter.

To enter, send:

(a) Completed and signed entry blank with correct category circled, br[...] description, techniques used, quilting method, and source of patter[...] design.

(b) Send two digital quilt images with **no modification** including croppi[...] and color correction (one full view of **completed** quilt and one detail [...] completed piece) on a CD-ROM, using a minimum of 4 MP (megapix[...] camera, on **highest resolution setting, saved as a jpeg or tiff file** (be su[...] to finish the CD and label the disk with your name and title of the work [...] Send only one entry per CD-ROM. If you have photos or slides of yo[...] work, you can have them saved on a CD-ROM at your local photo p[...] cessing center. Photos cannot be e-mailed, and CDs will not be return[...] Identifying name(s) must NOT be visible on the quilt in the images.

(c) Include a photo of the entrant(s) on the CD-ROM, so it will be availab[...] for the *American Quilter* magazine if you are a winner. The photo shou[...] include full face, head, and shoulders only.

(d) Entry fee:
    AQS members: $10.00 per quilt
    Non-members: $30.00 per quilt

Categories

Bed Quilts – width 60" to 110"; length 80" or more
1. Bed Quilts – Hand Quilted –quilting technique is by hand
2. Bed Quilts – Home Sewing Machine – predominant quilting technique is by home sewing machine
3. Bed Quilts – Longarm/Midarm Machine – predominant quilting technique is by longarm/midarm machine
4. 1st Entry in an AQS Quilt Contest – any technique
5. Group – any technique; made by three or more people

Handmade Quilts – width 60" to 110"; length 80" or more
6. Hand – any technique; the entire quilt top must be stitched by hand; backing and binding may be stitched by machine. Long lengthwise construction seams on the front may be machine stitched.

Large Wall Quilts – width 60" to 110"; length 40" or more
7. Large Wall Quilts – Hand Quilted – quilting technique is by hand
8. Large Wall Quilts – Home Sewing Machine – predominant quilting technique is by home sewing machine
9. Large Wall Quilts – Longarm/Midarm Machine – predominant quilting technique is by longarm/midarm machine
10. Pictorial Quilts–representation of a person, place, or thing – any technique

Small Wall Quilts – width 40" to 60"; length 40" or more
11. Small Wall Quilts – Hand Quilted – quilting technique is by hand
12. Small Wall Quilts – Home or Longarm/Midarm Sewing Machine – predominant quilting technique is by home or longarm/midarm sewing machine
13. Pictorial Quilts–representation of a person, place, or thing – any technique
14. 1st Entry in an AQS Quilt Contest – any technique

Young Designer Quilts – width 40" or more; length 40" or more
15. Young Designer – any technique in unique interpretation, open to ages 18 to 35 (determined on opening day of show)

Miniature Quilts – width 24" maximum; length 24" maximum
16. Miniature – all aspects of the quilt are in reduced scale

2009 AQS Quilt Show – Paducah
Entry Blank to Accompany CD-ROM (this form may be photocopied)

Member $10.00   ❏ Non-member $30.00   Membership # _____

Entrant's or Group Name _____

          (Please print)   (This name will be used in the Show Book.)

Street _____

City _____ State _____ Country _____ Zip or Postal Code _____

E-mail _____ Phone _____ Fax _____

Complete Name of Newspaper _____ Newspaper E-mail _____

Newspaper Mailing Address _____
        Street   City   State/Country   Zip/Postal Code

Circle One Category Number (see rule 10 for size):

Bed Quilts:
W 60" to 110"; L 80" or more
1. Hand Quilted
2. Home Sewing Machine
3. Longarm/Midarm Machine
4. 1st Entry – AQS Contest
5. Group

Handmade Quilts:
W 60" to 110"; L 80" or more
6. Hand

Large Wall Quilts:
W 60" to 110"; L 40" or more
7. Hand Quilted
8. Home Sewing Machine
9. Longarm/Midarm Machine
10. Pictorial Quilts

Small Wall Quilts
W 40" to 60"; L 40" or more
11. Hand Quilted
12. Home Sewing or Longarm/Midarm Machine
13. Pictorial Quilts
14. 1st Entry – AQS Contest

Young Designer Quilts
W 40" or more"; L 40" or more
15. Young Designer
Birthdate_____
Miniature
24" maximum, W and L
16. Miniature

Information about your entry:

Title _____ Size in inches _____ " across x _____ " long

Approx. Insurance Value $ _____ (Over $1,000 requires a written appraisal, maximum value $5,000)

Name(s) of everyone who stitched on this quilt: _____

_____

Brief Description of Quilt for Show Booklet (25 words) _____

_____

Techniques: (Choose all that apply)
❏ Appliqué   ❏ Piecing   ❏ Embroidery   ❏ Trapunto   ❏ Needlework Technique _____   ❏ Other _____

Quilting: (Choose all that apply)
  ❏ **Hand**   ❏ **Home Sewing Machine**   ❏ **Longarm/Midarm Machine**   ❏ **Embroidery Machine**
           ❏ with Stitch Regulator   ❏ with Stitch Regulator
                                ❏ Computer-Assisted Stitch Software

Design Pattern Source (Choose all that apply: Use separate paper for additional space)
❏ Totally Original (Definition: first, not a copy of a previous work; new creation; patterns by others are **not** used)
❏ Pattern(s) used; list pattern source (if any patterns were used, please list them below).

_____ _____ _____ _____
Magazine   Issue   Year   Project Title

_____ _____ _____ _____
Pattern/Book title – List complete title   Author   Publisher   Project Title

_____ _____
Other artwork title/type   Contact information for artist, publisher, or source

_____ _____
Workshop title   Workshop instructor

I wish to enter the above item and agree to abide by the quilt contest rules and decisions of the jury and judges. I understand that AQS will take every precaution to protect my quilt exhibited in this show. I realize they cannot be responsible for the acts of nature or others beyond their control. If my quilt is exhibited in the American Quilter's Society Show, I understand that my signature gives AQS the right to use a photo of my quilt for promotion of the AQS Quilt Show in any publications, advertisements, catalogue of Show Quilts, non-printable CD-ROM of show images, and other printed or electronic materials. AQS will request permission before using quilt for any other commercial purpose.

Please put your name on CD-ROM and mail digital images (as outlined in the rules), completed entry blank, and fee for each quilt to:

American Quilter's Society,
Dept. Paducah 2009 Entry,
PO Box 3290, Paducah, KY 42002-3290

Signature _____

Credit Card (Visa, MasterCard, or Discover)   Card Number ☐☐☐☐–☐☐☐☐–☐☐☐☐–☐☐☐☐   Exp. Date ☐☐☐☐   Ver. Code ☐☐☐☐   Check # _____

AQS presents the sponsors for the 24th Annual Quilt Show & Contest. Each catagory and event is sponsored by a company in the quilting industry. To open the show, company representatives present the cash awards at the Awards Presentation on Tuesday evening.

Best of Show . . . . **American Quilter's Society**

Hand Workmanship Award . . . . **American Quilter's Society**

Machine Workmanship Award . . . **Bernina of America, Inc.**

Longarm Machine Quilting Award . **Gammill Quilting Machine Co.**

Best Wall Quilt Award . . . . . . **Moda Fabrics**

Wall Hand Workmanship Award . . **Coats & Clark**

Wall Machine Workmanship Award **Brother International Corporation**

Wall Longarm Workmanship Award **Handi Quilter**

Olfa Young Designers Okada Award **Olfa Corporation**

Best Miniature Quilt. . . . . **Benartex, Inc.**

Bed Quilts

    Appliqué . . . . **Mountain Mist**

    Pieced . . . . **Hobbs Bonded Fibers**

    Mixed Techniques . . . . . . **EZ Quilting by Wrights**

    1st Entry in AQS Quilt Contest . **Morgan Quality Products**

    Group . . . . **Mettler**

Handmade Quilts . . . . **Hoffman California Fabrics**

Large Wall Quilts

    Appliqué . . . . **Fairfield Processing Corporation**

    Pieced . . . . **Baby Lock USA**

    Mixed Techniques . . . . . . **Robert Kaufman Co., Inc.**

    Pictorial . . . . **C & T Publishing**

Small Wall Quilts

    Traditional . . . . **FreeSpirit/Westminster Fabrics**

    Non-traditional . . . . **Koala Cabinets**

    Pictorial . . . . **Husqvarna Viking**

    1st Entry in AQS Quilt Contest . **YLI Corporation**

Young Designers . . . . **Olfa Corporation**

Miniature Quilts. . . . . **Benartex, Inc.**

Judges' Recognition . . . . **Possibilities**

Booth Hop . . . . **Benartex, Inc.**

Event Sponsors . . . . **Baby Lock USA, Ken's Sewing Center, Quilt in a Day**

Fashion Show. . . . . **AQS, Hobbs Bonded Fibers, Bernina of America, Inc.**

General Sponsors . . . . **A-1 Quilting Machines, AccuCut, Amazing Designs,**

. . . . **American Professional Designs, American Professional Quilting Systems,**

. . . . **Elna USA, Horn of America, PC Quilter, Statler Stitcher,**

. . . . **Superior Threads, TinLizzzie 18**

Lecture Series. . . . . **Pfaff Sales & Marketing**

Quilter's Park . . . . **Hinterberg Design**

Workshops . . . . **Bernina of America, Inc., Elan USA, Handi Quilter, Janome America, Inc., Pfaff, TinLizzie 18**

MAQS Workshop Series . . . . . . **Flynn Quilt Frames, Janome America, Olfa Corporation**

MAQS Sawtooth Contest. . . . . . **Clover Needlecraft, Inc., Fairfield Processing Corporation, Janome America, Inc.**